OVER THE TOP

OVER THE TOP

Discover God's Extravagant Love

Margaret Feinberg

Foreword by Mary Graham

THOMAS NELSON
Since 1798

NASHVILLE   DALLAS   MEXICO CITY   RIO DE JANEIRO

Published in Nashville, Tennessee, by Thomas Nelson. Thomas Nelson is a trademark of Thomas Nelson, Inc.

Thomas Nelson, Inc., titles may be purchased in bulk for educational, business, fund-raising, or sales promotional use. For information, please e-mail SpecialMarkets@ThomasNelson.com.

ISBN: 978-1-4185-4185-9

Printed in China

10 11 12 13 14 MT 5 4 3 2 1

Contents

Contents

Foreword

As a freshman in high school, I memorized a book by Dr. Seuss called *Thidwick the Big-Hearted Moose*. These many years later, I smile as I remember that wonderful children's story, which I committed to memory during a forensic tournament and recited over and over again.

The story was about Thidwick, a moose who had big horns and an even bigger heart. As his friends (first flies, then birds, then bears, as I recall) began to notice those enormous horns, they started asking for a little ride. By the end of the story, poor Thidwick had so many residents on his head he could barely stand up straight.

Interestingly, I love that story now as much as I did then. Sometimes I, like Thidwick, don't know where to stop. Seeing the needs of others, it's easy for me to overextend my capacity. Unfortunately, I take on too much, laying all wisdom aside. Maybe that's why someone recently gave me a notepad that says "SOS" at the top with this new interpretation: "Seriously Over Scheduled." That was the moose's problem, and it's often mine.

In our humanity it's easy to project that "weakness" onto God when, in reality, He has unlimited capacity. There's always more love, more grace, more kindness, more generosity, more forgiveness; more of what we could ever need or desire.

Not just childhood fantasies, but also our own realities and experience teach us to limit our expectations, hold back on our desires, reframe our needs, and discipline ourselves to settle for less. We're taught early on to manage our deficiencies. As children of the living God, however, I challenge you to open your heart to a new way of thinking. Perhaps there is enough, even more than enough. When Scripture teaches God's love is perfect, His forgiveness unending, His grace eternal, and His desire for us more than we can think or imagine . . . we can believe it.

But these "lofty" thoughts cannot take root in our hearts by hoping, wishing, or dreaming. They become reality only as we dive deeply into the Word of God, letting His Spirit teach us the height and depth of His love and the extent of His grace and forgiveness.

How does God manage to provide all this great care to His children? Often He uses us. Mysteriously, His love, grace, forgiveness, and provision flow through us to meet the needs of others. Not because we try harder but because His love flows freely. We don't have to give beyond our limitations as my friend the moose did, but as we have been given. That's what excites me about this study. Look into God's Word to see and know what His desire is for you . . . and how once His love is received, it flows freely through you to others. It's not like anything we've ever seen or known. His love is truly *Over the Top* and beyond our imaginations.

—MARY GRAHAM

Introduction

Overflowing with Adoration

Remember when you were young and received a sweet gift—a box of chocolates or a bag of yummy candy? Odds are one of your parents or a loving grandparent warned you that eating the entire gift wasn't such a great idea; if you ate too many too quickly, you wouldn't feel well afterward. But sometimes it was hard to resist and you suffered the consequences of your overindulgence—a tummy ache and an "I told you so!" The candy that had seemed so delectable and desirable made you feel nauseous and ill. It also taught you that too much of a good thing can be a bad thing.

While that basic life principle remains true for many things, including eating, shopping, and even working, it doesn't hold true when it comes to our relationship with God. God is overflowing with adoration for each of us. The love God has for us cannot be contained. If you tried to stuff the love of God into a box or canister, the top would literally pop off! The love of God cannot be packed away. God's love is simply beyond our comprehension. It's literally over the top!

Just as God is overflowing with love for us, we are invited to live lives that overflow with love for Him. We are invited to worship, adore, and give thanks without limit to God. We have the opportunity to give ourselves, our whole selves, to Him and hold nothing back. We can fill our lives to overflowing with God's love. Unlike a box of candy, God will never make our tummies sick; instead, we'll find ourselves hungry for more of Him.

God wants to reveal Himself to each of us in fresh and new ways. Whether you're just getting to know God for the first time or you've been a follower of God for many years, He still has something new He wants to reveal to you. God goes over the top when it comes to giving us His abounding grace, uncontainable love, and renewed hope. My hope and prayer for you are that, through this study, you will discover God in a fresh way that reignites your faith and love for Him. In the process, may you recognize God as being over the top in your own life.

Blessings,

Margaret Feinberg

A God
Without Limits

This section describes the fullness of life that abounds

when we allow God to reign in us. God is bursting at

the seams with surprises for our hearts and lives—things

beyond our wildest imaginations. In order to enter into

the fullness of all God has for us, we need to examine and

erase the lines we've drawn in our relationships with Him.

One

Popping with Surprises

The love of Christ both wounds and heals, it fascinates and frightens, it kills and makes alive, it draws and repulses. There can be nothing more terrible or wonderful than to be stricken with love for Christ so deeply that the whole being goes out in a pained adoration of His person, an adoration that disturbs and disconcerts while it purges and satisfies and relaxes the deep inner heart.

A. W. TOZER

One lazy Sunday afternoon, Mariam found herself with a craving for popcorn. Instead of simply heating up a bag of microwave popcorn as she had on previous weekends, Mariam decided she wanted to do it the old-fashioned way: she chose to make stovetop popcorn. She pulled a frying pan out of a kitchen cabinet, placed it on the stove, and slowly heated the vegetable oil. When the oil began to simmer, she added a small handful of kernels. She watched with delight, impatiently waiting for the kernels to pop. The pan continued to heat. She looked around the kitchen for a lid for the pan. Unable to find one, she decided she wouldn't need one.

Unfortunately, Mariam failed to take into account the name of the food she was preparing—POPcorn. After a few minutes of waiting, she watched as the kernels of corn went flying in all directions, even overflowing onto the floor. Rather than be upset at her miscalculation, she found herself laughing at the entire scene. For months to come, Mariam found popcorn, as well as unpopped kernels, all around her house. Each one was a reminder that popcorn in an open pan just can't be contained!

God often uses the little seeds of His Word to make big changes in our lives.

Mariam's story is a simple but powerful glimpse into what can happen when we take the lid off all God wants to do in our lives. Like popcorn in a heated, open pan, God is not one to be contained. He wants access to all our hearts and our entire lives, even into the crevices and areas where we may not see Him working right away. Like Mariam's popcorn kernels, God often uses the little seeds of His Word to make big changes in our lives. As those seeds grow, we find ourselves changing in unexpected ways. We find ourselves loving, giving, and serving in areas we never expected. At times, God will call us to do things we think are difficult, if not impossible; but He is with us every step of the way. Indeed, God is always popping with surprises.

1. Have you ever had a kitchen mishap like Mariam's? What happened? What was the result?

2. In what ways has God been popping into your life lately? How has He been surprising you with His presence in everyday life?

3. In the space below, describe a time when you felt God was lifting the lid off His relationship with you. What was the result?

God's love and care for us exceed our wildest imaginations. Need proof? Just consider the apostle Paul. In his early life, Paul (then named Saul) imprisoned Christians and did everything he could to destroy the early church. God stepped into Paul's life, and he was transformed forever. Paul is now known as the Apostle to the Gentiles (non-Jews). In his letter to the church in Ephesus, Paul prayed that the Ephesians would praise God for His awesome work as seen in His Son, Jesus Christ.

4. Read **Ephesians 3:14–21**.What did Paul specifically pray for in this passage? Make a list of his requests in the space below. Do you ever pray these things for others? Why or why not?

5. What was Paul in awe of in **Ephesians 3:20**?

6. In what ways have you found the things Paul described in this verse to be true in your own life?

7. *Are there any ways in which you have been putting a lid on something God wants to do in your life? Explain in the space below.*

8. *What steps can you take to remove the lid, or limitations, you may have placed on God's work in you?*

God is over the top when it comes to His love for you. His work in and through you is greater than anything you can imagine.

Digging Deeper

In Philippians 4:11–13, Paul explained how he found a way to be content in all circumstances. Reflecting on this passage, who was it that gave Paul strength? How have you found this true in your own life?

Bonus Activity

Write *Philippians 4:11–13* on a series of note cards or sticky notes. Post them anywhere and everywhere around your house, workplace, and car. Use this passage as a reminder of God's infinite strength.

Two

Coloring Outside the Lines

God loves you right where you are, but
he doesn't want to leave you there.

Max Lucado

Ann remembers the first time she encountered a state line on a road trip with her parents. She was in fifth grade and had just spent an entire semester memorizing the names of all the different states and their capitals. The test at the end of the semester was difficult and challenging, yet she managed to earn a B+.

As Ann's family drove between North Carolina (state capital: Raleigh) and Florida (state capital: Tallahassee), Ann waited with great anticipation for the moment they would cross the border into Georgia (state capital: Atlanta). As they passed the large sign that welcomed them into Georgia, Ann stared at the picture of the big, juicy peach. Suddenly, she was grateful she didn't have to memorize all the state fruits.

Ann searched the ground for a state border. After months of studying the maps of the United States, she fully expected to see hand-painted borders between the states. Confused by the scene, she asked her mom where the black lines were located. Had she missed them? Her mom tenderly explained that the "Welcome to Georgia" sign was the only physical notice of a border between the states. Ann was upset. She figured since someone placed all those lines on a map and made fifth graders memorize all the details, the least government officials could do was put the same lines on the land. In her ten-year-old mind, a map should be fully representative of the land it describes.

God doesn't want to be held back by anything in our lives: not by fear, doubt, insecurity, pride, bitterness, or anger.

Looking back on the situation, Ann laughs and admits she had a lot to learn about topography. But she also says the lesson from that road trip years ago has stayed with her. She recognizes parallels in her own spiritual life. Ann says, "In my desire to know God, I have discovered lots of black, painted lines in my own life. Like the lines on maps, these lines are more a result of perception than reality. God is welcome only in some areas of my soul. I welcome Him into my gratitude and even my repentance, but I shut the door when He wants to go deeper into my doubts, fears, and innermost thoughts. I welcome Him into a Sunday morning service but quickly forget Him when I'm pumping gas on the ride home later that afternoon. It's as if I have these thin black lines drawn throughout my little world of where God is and where He's not, forgetting that He's everywhere."

Ann says that she is slowly learning to erase the lines she has drawn in her relationship with God. In the process, she is discovering that God wants an all-access pass to her life. Just as in Ann's life, God doesn't want to be held back by anything in our lives: not by fear, doubt, insecurity, pride, bitterness, or anger. He wants full access to our hearts and our lives.

1. *While lines on a map are easy to see, it's much more difficult to recognize boundaries we may have put in place in our relationship with God. Can you think of any areas in which you recognize a boundary or line you've drawn in your relationship with God? If so, write it down in the heart shape below:*

2. *What are some of the causes of drawn lines in your relationship with God? (Examples: disappointment, frustration, etc.)*

3. *What is the result of drawing a line in your relationship with God? Whom do you think the line hurts more—you or God?*

Unlike states, God doesn't need boundaries to tell Him where to be—He is everywhere. He is unlimited. In King David's well-known Psalm 139, he mixes praise and wisdom to describe the unending qualities of God.

*4. Read **Psalm 139**. How would you describe the tone of this psalm?*

5. What emotions are evoked as you read this passage?

There is no place so high, deep, or wide that it is beyond God's reach.

6. *In the charts below, draw a line from each reference to its matching Scripture:*

Reference
Job 42:2
Psalm 115:3
Matthew 19:26
Luke 1:37

Scripture
"With man this is impossible, but with God all things are possible."
"I know that you can do all things; no plan of yours can be thwarted."
"For nothing is impossible with God."
Our God is in heaven; he does whatever pleases him.

7. *Reflecting on the Scriptures in the above chart, do you think drawing lines in your relationship with God is a healthy or unhealthy way to live? Explain.*

8. *By removing the boundaries in your relationship with God, what can you expect to be different? Explain.*

God wants us to walk in wholeness. In His love, God wants to erase every line that separates us from Him.

Digging Deeper

David knew what it felt like to have a crushed spirit. Psalm 34 is connected to a time in David's life when he was forced to fake madness to escape the courts of the Philistines (1 Samuel 21:10–15). Read Psalm 34:18. In what ways is it comforting for you to feel God near? Have there been times in your life when you have been broken-hearted and crushed in spirit and experienced God's presence? How has God's presence been a source of comfort for you?

Bonus Activity

Over the course of the next week, make some time to spend alone with God in prayer. Specifically ask God to reveal any lines you've drawn in your relationship with Him. On a piece of paper, write any revelation you sense from God's Spirit. Ask God to help you remove anything blocking you from a closer relationship with Him. Then shred the list of boundaries as a symbol of the work He is doing in your heart.

Three

Grace Abounding

*Love that goes upward is worship; love that goes
outward is affection; love that stoops is grace.*

Donald Grey Barnhouse

When we hear the name "La Guardia," many of us think of the
smaller airport in New York City. However, the airport was built by
Mayor Fiorello La Guardia—also small (under 5'5")—during his term
as mayor of New York City. Originally named Floyd Bennett Field,
it was later renamed LaGuardia Airport. Mayor La Guardia lived
a legacy. Serving during the Great Depression and World War II,
he had a lot to fix in New York City. He took a hard stance against
crime, supported the New Deal, and looked out for the good of the
people. He is even remembered for reading the comics to children
over the radio during a newspaper strike.

On a frigid night in 1935, La Guardia traveled to a neighborhood
night court to serve as magistrate in one of the poorest parts of the
city. One of the cases over which he presided that evening involved
an elderly woman who had been charged with stealing a loaf of bread

from a local vendor. The vendor wanted justice to prevail in the case of this woman who would dare to steal from him. He also wanted the community to be taught a lesson about what happens to thieves. When La Guardia asked why she stole the bread, the woman told the mayor about her life. Her son-in-law had left her daughter with two kids to care for. Her daughter was ill and her family was literally starving. Being penniless, the woman felt she had no choice; she had to take the bread for her family to survive.

One of the most generous displays of God's grace is His invitation to know Jesus and accept the free gift of eternal life.

After a few moments of silence, La Guardia stood up and announced to the court that the woman had to be punished. He told them he didn't have a choice; the law must be enforced. Then the mayor reached into his wallet and pulled out a ten-dollar bill—the amount of the elderly woman's fine. In addition to paying her fine, La Guardia fined everyone in the courtroom fifty cents for contributing to a town where someone would feel the need to steal to end starvation. He asked the bailiff to collect the fine, even from the vendor, and present it to the woman. Stunned, she left that night with $47.50 in her pocket.

On that unforgettable winter night, Mayor La Guardia showed grace to the elderly woman. He extended overwhelming kindness to someone who didn't necessarily deserve it. He stooped down and poured out unmerited love, asking for nothing in return. God's grace is similar. Just as La Guardia showed grace to the elderly woman, God shows grace to us. We don't deserve God's grace; we deserve the penalty for our actions. Instead, God extends His unmerited favor toward us. One of the most generous displays of God's grace is His invitation to know Jesus and accept the free gift of eternal life. It's completely undeserved, but it's just one more demonstration of the abounding grace of God in our lives.

1. What is surprising about La Guardia's response to the woman in this story?

2. How do you think the people watching in the courtroom responded to La Guardia's ruling? The vendor? The woman?

3. Have you ever been in a situation in which you experienced grace and forgiveness like the woman in the story? If so, describe. How does it make you feel to receive something you know you don't deserve?

Unlike other religions, Christianity doesn't offer a way to buy entrance into heaven. You simply cannot purchase love from God. Instead, God gives His love freely. God extends grace to each of us.

In his letter to Titus, Paul described grace. He asked Titus to remind the people of Crete about God's wonderful grace—the undeserved salvation designed for blemished humans because of God's love for us.

4. Read *Titus 3:4–7* below. *Circle or underline the words* **kindness,** **love, mercy,** *and* **grace.**

> *But when the kindness and love of God our Savior appeared, he saved us, not because of righteous things we had done, but because of his mercy. He saved us through the washing of rebirth and renewal by the Holy Spirit, whom he poured out on us generously through Jesus Christ our Savior, so that, having been justified by his grace, we might become heirs having the hope of eternal life.*

Reflecting on **Titus 3:4–7,** *how does it make you feel to know that God did all of this for you? On a scale of 1 to 10, how difficult is it to accept the gift of His grace and love? What holds you back from fully accepting the gift of God's grace and love?*

Easy 1—2—3—4—5—6—7—8—9—10 Difficult

In his letter to the church in Ephesus, Paul wrote one of the clearest and best descriptions of salvation. He began Ephesians 2:1 by reminding everyone they were once "dead in [their] transgressions and sins." He went on to describe the new life available to us when we accept God's grace.

5. *Read* **Ephesians 2:4–9** *below. Circle or underline the words* **kindness, love, mercy,** *and* **grace.**

> But because of his great love for us, God, who is rich in mercy, made us alive with Christ even when we were dead in transgressions—it is by grace you have been saved. And God raised us up with Christ and seated us with him in the heavenly realms in Christ Jesus, in order that in the coming ages he might show the incomparable riches of his grace, expressed in his kindness to us in Christ Jesus. For it is by grace you have been saved, through faith—and this not from yourselves, it is the gift of God—not by works, so that no one can boast.

6. *According to this passage, what are some of the benefits of God's gift of grace?*

Not only is it important to accept God's grace through His Son, Jesus Christ, but it is also important that we extend grace to others.

7. *What are some ways you can replicate and extend the grace of God in everyday life?*

> *Grace is a free gift from God that cannot be earned or purchased. Through grace, not only do we have the opportunity to enter into a relationship with God, but we are saved and empowered to do good works.*

Digging Deeper

Read Ephesians 1:7–10. According to this passage, what has been lavished on each of us? We are called not only to accept God's grace, but also to live a life of grace. Toward whom can you show grace today?

Bonus Activity

Look for an opportunity to show grace to someone this week through an act of generous kindness. Give a gift. Perform an act of service. Offer a kind word. Write an encouraging note. Put your faith to work in a tangible way.

Overpowered by His Love

Nothing is as over the top as God's

love for us. It simply can't be contained.

It's beyond our comprehension.

When God's love floods our lives,

it changes everything within us.

Four

For God So Loved the World

Incomprehensible and immutable is the love of God.
For it was not after we were reconciled to him by
the blood of his Son that he began to love us, but
he loved us before the foundation of the world,
that with his only begotten Son we too might be
sons of God before we were anything at all.

AUGUSTINE OF HIPPO

Tony had been diagnosed with HIV. After years of wrestling with the disease, it had progressed to full-blown AIDS. As if his health was not a large enough source of constant worry and struggle, he found his life blown apart by another storm—Hurricane Katrina. He had lost everything. Broke and homeless, he sought refuge in a city farther west. After several weeks, he managed to secure inexpensive housing; but when he moved in he had nothing—no furniture, not even a bed.

One woman, Tamara, heard about his story and was compelled to do something. Though she and her family had always reached out to those less fortunate than themselves by taking meals to the hungry, supporting children in third world countries, and providing gifts for those in need, she had never gotten involved in a situation this close to home. Tamara decided to take her family shopping. Together they purchased a bed and new bedding and delivered it to Tony. He was shocked and overwhelmed by the act of kindness and generosity. He couldn't help but sob with tears of joy. He didn't care that complete strangers saw his tears.

Tamara was so moved by the experience she couldn't keep the story to herself. She shared it with others, including friends and fam-

> *No matter what you've done, nothing is beyond the love of God.*

ily, who also wanted to get involved. Soon after, Tamara's sister purchased new furniture for Tony's apartment. Church members heard about Tony's needs and bought new pots, pans, and cooking utensils. Gradually, Tony's apartment felt like a home. Tamara and her family got together and threw Tony a birthday party. As Tony felt more comfortable, he began to share bits of his life. That's when Tamara learned he was one of fourteen kids. His mom was still alive and well in Mississippi. He had daughters and grandchildren.

Over time, Tony's illness became worse. One day he walked to the emergency room and discovered there was nothing more they could do to help him. He was given less than four months to live. He could no longer keep his illness a secret. He decided to confide in Tamara, who had become like a big sister to him. When Tamara heard Tony's prognosis, she pleaded with him to allow her to contact his family. Tony finally agreed. To Tony's surprise, his family, overwhelmed by hearing from their long-lost son, welcomed him home with open arms. Tony eventually died in his sleep, surrounded by the love of his family.

Tony's story is a beautiful reminder that love wins. Not only did Tony experience the love of complete strangers through Tamara, her family, and the church, but he also experienced the love and acceptance of his own family. As powerful as these experiences of love were for Tony, they pale in comparison to God's love for us. His love is more powerful, stronger, and deeper than we can fathom. His love redeems our past and gives us hope for the future. No matter what you've done, nothing is beyond the love of God; He may use the most unexpected people and situations to reveal His love.

1. *Have you ever reached out to someone like Tony? What was your experience? How were you blessed and challenged by the experience?*

2. *It may not have been as dramatic, but have you ever been in a situation like Tony's where others reached out and expressed the love of God to you? If so, describe. What did you learn through the experience?*

Just as Tony's family welcomed him home, God is always willing to receive us back into His embrace. Although we may feel unworthy, God's grace paves the way for us to return to His waiting, open arms. If you doubt, remember the story of the prodigal son.

*3. Read **Luke 15:11–32**. Fill in the chart below with the reactions surrounding the younger son's return. (For the reactions of some, you may need to use your imagination.)*

Person	Reaction
Younger Son	(vv. 18–19)
Father	(v. 20)
Older Brother	(vv. 28–30)
Servants	(vv. 22–24)

This famous parable is sometimes titled "The Prodigal Son," but many also refer to it as "The Forgiving Father." Luke 15:20 says, "While he was still a long way off, his father saw him and was filled with compassion for him; he ran to his son, threw his arms around him and kissed him."

4. During the course of your life, you might have felt similarly to one of the characters in this story. Consider the following:

Have you ever felt like the prodigal son? Describe.

Have you ever felt like the older brother? Describe.

Have you ever felt like the father? Describe.

5. The father must have had a hunch that his son would take the money, leave, and squander it. Why do you think the father allowed his son to travel down that path?

6. The younger son in this story was tempted to take everything he could and run away. Have you ever faced this temptation personally? Have you ever known someone who behaved like the younger brother? Explain.

7. Have you ever been in the situation of being forced to learn from your own bad decision? What was the outcome?

8. What parallels do you see between God and the father described in this story? In what ways have you experienced God as your loving and forgiving Father?

God so loves the world that nothing is beyond His redemption or restoration. Like the father in the story of the prodigal son, God is a forgiving Father who wants to see us come home to a relationship with Him.

Digging Deeper

Read John 3:1–21. What was the setting in which Jesus gave us the famous passage of John 3:16–17? Whom did Jesus come to save? How does knowing God's heart for the world affect the way you see and treat others?

Bonus Activity

Intentionally look for an opportunity to meet the needs of someone like Tony. Buy a homeless person a gift certificate for a hot meal. Offer to volunteer an afternoon at a food bank. Look for the opportunity this week to get involved in the immediate needs of your community.

Five

Multidimensional Love

He who counts the stars and calls them by
their names is in no danger of forgetting
His own children. He knows your case as
thoroughly as if you were the only creature He
ever made or the only saint He ever loved.

C. H. SPURGEON

Who knew that one man's passion could help hundreds of people in need? Hal Colston worked at a local agency in Vermont dedicated to assisting low-income clients. He was frustrated by the amount of poverty and lack of assistance the lower-class people in his area were experiencing. Though many could secure jobs, they were unable to provide themselves transportation to and from work. Without a reliable car or a ride, many soon lost their jobs. The pattern was relentlessly repeated.

One woman's story sent Colston over the edge. The woman came to him in tears. She had recently purchased a car for $500, but it broke down before she got it home. The seller refused to refund her money. Because she had no way to drive to and from work, she was fired from her job. As a single mother, she could no longer afford to care for her two young daughters. She was at her wit's end. Hal felt compelled to do something about her dire situation.

In 2004 Colston, along with a few of his church friends, funded an organization called Good News Garage. The local community garage accepts the donation of broken-down and damaged cars, fixes them, and matches them with families in need. As a result, families can purchase a car that is not only affordable, but reliable and safe. Colston's attempt to make a difference began in Vermont but quickly spread to Connecticut, Massachusetts, New Hampshire, and Rhode Island. Hal Colston was so passionate about assisting low-income people that he formed an organization specifically designed to aid them. Colston stepped out on a limb to fight poverty in his area and ended up helping people throughout the northeastern United States. God wants us to be conduits of His love to others.

God wants us to be conduits of His love to others.

1. *Hal Colston found an opportunity to help people in need. What opportunities exist in your community for you to make a difference? What could your study group do together to make a difference?*

As we begin to understand the dimensions of God's love, we are better able to show that kind of love to others.

2. *In the space below, write five words that come to mind when you consider God's multidimensional love.*

3. *Look up each of the following Scriptures and write down the description of God's love from each verse.*

Scripture	Description of God's Love
John 15:13	It is a self-sacrificing love!
Romans 8:35	
John 14:23	
Ephesians 6:24	
Jeremiah 31:3	

4. *Which of these Scriptures is the most encouraging to you? Which of these Scriptures is the most challenging to you? Which Scriptures about God's love, besides the ones listed above, are particularly meaningful to you?*

In Luke 10:25–37, a lawyer asked Jesus how to inherit eternal life. The lawyer knew he must love God and his neighbor, but he asked Jesus exactly who qualified as his "neighbor." With whom was he to share God's love? As on other occasions, Jesus used a parable to respond to the man's question.

5. Read **Luke 10:25–37**. Why might the priest and the Levite in the parable have passed by the injured man?

The distance between Jerusalem and Jericho was seventeen miles. The only road linking the two cities was treacherous—a well-known hideout for thieves. But those wishing to make the journey were forced to walk the dangerous path. A modern-day comparison would be to take a nighttime stroll through a gang-ridden, inner-city area.

6. The Samaritan in the story went out of his way to take care of the man who was left for dead. Reread **Luke 10:33–35** below. Circle or underline all the verbs used by Jesus to describe the actions of the Samaritan.

"But a Samaritan, as he traveled, came where the man was; and when he saw him, he took pity on him. He went to him and bandaged his wounds, pouring on oil and wine. Then he put the man on his own donkey, took him to an inn and took care of *him. The next day he took out two silver coins and gave them to the innkeeper. 'Look after him,' he said, 'and when I return, I will reimburse you for any extra expense you may have.'"*

The Samaritan didn't just stop to help the man; he ensured his recovery. Historically, Jews looked down upon Samaritans. Jesus' choice of a Samaritan as the hero of the story was shocking.

7. *Does anything surprise you about the involvement of the Samaritan in the attacked man's life? Who would be comparable to a modern-day Samaritan in our culture? Is there anything more the Samaritan could have done?*

8. *In **Luke 10:37**, we are asked to "go and do likewise." How would reflecting the values of the Samaritan in Jesus' parable look in your everyday life?*

God's love is multidimensional. His love isn't just given to us; it's meant to flow through us to others.

Digging Deeper

We can express our love for God in many different ways. Read Mark 12:30. What dimensions of love are mentioned in this verse? How can you more fully love God in each of those four expressions?

Bonus Activity

Make a list of people who have made a difference in your life. Over the course of the next week, express your gratitude to at least three of them. Send a letter. Write an e-mail. Pick up the phone. By letting others know how much they've encouraged you, you'll be encouraging them to continue serving others.

Six

Uncontainable Love

I am so washed in the tide of His measureless love that I seem to be below the surface of a sea and cannot touch or see or feel anything around me except its water.

CATHERINE OF GENOA

Some ideas are just hard to wrap our minds around. Think about eternity. How long does eternity last? Forever. That's an unimaginable time. Now think about something that's uncontainable, something too vast to be limited or enclosed. That, too, is a concept beyond our ability to understand. Yet both words describe God's love for each of us; God's love is eternal and simply uncontainable.

The truth is, God doesn't want you to just be aware of His love or even just captivated by it. He wants His love to saturate you. He wants you so filled up with His love that it pours from you. First John 3:1 says, "How great is the love the Father has lavished on us, that we should be called children of God! And that is what we are!" As children of God, we have an amazing opportunity and invitation to share that love with others. Does God's uncontainable love flow in and through you? Take the following quiz to find out:

The Uncontainable Love Quiz

For each numbered item, check the comment that best describes you:

1	☐ I jump at the opportunity to serve others.	☐ I hesitate to get involved.
2	☐ I am excited about how God can use me.	☐ I'm unsure of what God wants.
3	☐ I feel active and involved.	☐ I feel lonely and isolated.
4	☐ I make time for others.	☐ I'm too busy for quality time.
5	☐ I feel God's love alive inside me.	☐ God seems distant.
6	☐ I take time to pray each day.	☐ I pray as a last resort.
7	☐ I think my best days are ahead of me.	☐ I think my best days are past.
8	☐ I look for God-infused moments each day.	☐ I rarely see God in life.
9	☐ I feel joyful about life.	☐ I dread waking up each day.
10	☐ I want God to work in and through me.	☐ I wonder where God is.

If you have more checks in the left-hand column, God's love is alive within you. You're watchful for the ways God wants to pour His love in and through you, and you recognize your need of Him each day. God's uncontainable love can't help but flow out of you.

If you have more checks in the right-hand column, you can be sure God wants to do more in and through you. He longs for you to experience His love in ways you've never seen before. He isn't giving you His love so you can keep it, but so you can give it away to others. When you find yourself discouraged, remember that God has a hope and a future for you beyond anything you can imagine.

1. *Which column did you check most often? Do any of your answers in the quiz surprise you? Explain.*

2. *In what circumstances do you find it hard to show love to others? In what circumstances do you find it easy to show love to others? Explain.*

Paul wrote two letters to the church in Corinth. In his first, he addressed love. Paul used the Greek word *agape* to describe the divine love found through Christ. This is significant because *agape* was rarely used in speech at the time, except when describing a god-like love. During this time the word typically used for love was the Greek word *philia*, which describes a friendship or companionship love. *Agape* surpasses *philia* because it is the pure and holy love found in a relationship with Christ.

3. Read *1 Corinthians 13:1–3*. What can you accomplish without love? What specific examples does Paul use to get this point across?

4. Read *1 Corinthians 13:4–8*. Using this passage, fill in the chart below, noting everything that love **is**, as well as everything that love **is not**.

Love is . . .	Love is not . . .
Patient	Envious

*After filling in this chart, reread 1 **Corinthians** 13:4–8, replacing the word **love** with the name of our Lord, Jesus. (Example: **Jesus** is patient, **Jesus** is kind . . .) How does this substitution change the meaning of this passage for you?*

5. *Read 1 **Corinthians** 13:13. What three things does Paul say endure forever? Why do you think Paul chose love as the greatest?*

The apostle Paul wanted the church in Ephesus to know how deeply and desperately God loved them. He wanted them to be able to comprehend the love of Christ. Paul knew that when they loved God and experienced the fullness of God's love, some of the other struggles and issues they were wrestling with would disappear.

6. *Read **Ephesians** 3:17–19. According to Paul, what is it that surpasses knowledge? Do you find this to be true in your own life?*

7. What does it mean to you to be "rooted and established in love" (v. 17)?

8. The Bible tells us to walk in love. How can you show God's love toward others in every action, thought, or word?

God's love is uncontainable. It is meant to flow out of our lives in every direction—even when we least expect it. When we experience God's love personally, we are in the best place to share His love with others.

Digging Deeper

In his letter to Colosse, Paul told the people how to live in relationship with one another. Read Colossians 3:12–14. What did Paul direct us to give one another? How can you more fully love people by following these guidelines?

Bonus Activity

Head to your local library. Check out Gary Chapman's book *The Five Love Languages*. Chapman postulates that there are five different ways people understand and express love. Through these "love languages"—words of affirmation, quality time, gifts, acts of service, and physical touch—people can more fully learn to love others. Prayerfully consider your own love language, as well as the love languages of those around you, and determine how you can best show an uncontainable love that others will understand.

Compelled by His Generosity

Our God is over the top in so many ways, including

His generosity. By His very nature, God is constantly

giving. He gives us life and breath and hope. He

provides for us even when we don't realize our

need. Indeed, our God is outrageously generous.

Seven

Amazingly Generous

God cannot give us a happiness and
peace apart from Himself, because it is
not there. There is no such thing.

C. S. LEWIS

He was a racecar driver, world-renowned actor, and food company founder—can you guess this man's name? He was born in a small Ohio town, and success didn't seem to be in his future. His father owned and operated a sporting goods store, where his mother also worked. He attended high school and developed a passion for acting. (In fact, his first role was playing an extra in his high school's production of *Robin Hood*.) After serving in the navy during World War II, he went on to finish his college degree—in drama. Today we know him as the star of such movies as *The Color of Money* and *Cool Hand Luke*.

Who is it? Paul Newman. He touched America's heart with his gift for acting and, even more so, with his giving attitude. In 1982 Paul and a friend founded the company Newman's Own. Over the years it evolved into a large corporation, now known for the production of all-natural goodies, such as Newman-O's and various salad dressings. When the company was first founded, Newman pledged 100 percent of the profits from Newman's Own to nonprofit organizations. Since its start, Newman's Own has donated more than $250 million to various nonprofits. On September 26, 2008, Paul Newman died of cancer. Newman's Own continues to donate all their profits.

The Association of Hole in the Wall Camps is one of the nonprofits that receives funding from Newman's Own. Newman himself founded this organization and named it after the hideout in his movie *Butch Cassidy and the Sundance Kid*. This organization provides a camping experience, free of charge, for children with serious or terminal illnesses. It even offers a special program for hospitalized children. These experiences offer children a chance to regain some of the childhood they have lost to disease. They have a chance to put their illnesses in the background and just have fun!

When you reflect on just how generous God is, you can't help but experience gratitude and share that generosity with others.

You don't have to be a famous actor or own a company to live a life of generosity. Every day, we each have the opportunity to give in the places we live, work, and play. Giving can be as simple as picking a neighbor some flowers from your yard, taking someone who is discouraged to lunch for some good conversation and laughter, or baking some cookies for a shut-in. But a truly generous heart isn't something you can fashion on your own. Real generosity is found in the knowledge that you could never give as much as God has given you. When you reflect on just how generous God is, you can't help but experience gratitude and share that generosity with others.

1. Did anything surprise you about Paul Newman's story? Explain.

2. If you could make a difference through one organization or ministry, which one would it be?

In almost every letter the apostle Paul wrote, the introduction contained a prayer. Every letter's prayer hinted at the problems Paul was going to address in the rest of his letter. The prayer in his letter to Ephesus is unlike the others because it actually contains a long blessing. In Ephesians 1, Paul expressed the wonders of salvation found in Jesus Christ.

3. Read *Ephesians 1:3–10*. In the chart below, list the things described in this passage that God has done for us.

God's Overwhelming Actions
(v. 3) Blessed us in the heavenly realms with every spiritual blessing in Christ
(v. 4)
(v. 5)
(v. 6)
(v. 7)
(v. 8)
(v. 9)

4. Does anything about the list in the chart above surprise you? How often do you think about all the things God has done for you?

5. Think of three times in your life when you have seen God work in overwhelmingly generous ways. Describe in the space below.

God blesses us generously. In 2 Corinthians, we are asked to be just like God—cheerful givers.

6. Read *2 Corinthians 9:6–11*. *What do we receive when we are cheerful givers?*

7. *How have you found this to be true in your own life?*

We should not give with reluctance; verse 7 tells us, "God loves a cheerful giver." By being completely committed to God, we are able to give with happy hearts because we know God will take care of us!

8. *No matter how generous you already are, what would it look like for you to bump up your level of generosity one more notch? What steps can you take to give with a truly cheerful heart?*

> *God is amazingly generous to each of us, and we have the opportunity to reflect that generosity to others. God does not want us to give out of guilt or compulsion, but with a cheerful heart that honors Him.*

Digging Deeper

We don't have to fear being generous, because God is our provider. Psalm 72 is one of the two psalms ascribed to King Solomon, King David's son. In this passage, Solomon addressed the coming King of kings—Jesus. Read Psalm 72:12–13. Solomon was anticipating the arrival of a compassionate King. What actions are attributed to Jesus in this passage? Have you ever felt like the weak, needy, or afflicted in this passage? Did you cry out to Jesus? Describe the outcome.

Bonus Activity

Sit down with your family and look over the family's budget. Are there areas in which you could cut back in order to provide for someone in need? Pray for a cheerful heart as you look for additional ways to give generously to others.

Eight

Nothing Is Beyond Restoration

We are the healers who can reach
out and offer health, and we are all
patients in constant need of help.

HENRI NOUWEN

A group of missionaries was ministering in the Philippines. In order to get away and take a break, they vacationed in the city of Baguio and enjoyed the beautiful forests and waterfalls there. One day the group decided to tour a school where silversmiths were trained. As they walked through the building, they admired the various master-pieces under construction. The workers formed their artwork with cool metal instead of hot metal like blacksmiths. Each piece of art was carefully chiseled and designed into something wonderful. Near the end of the tour, they visited the gift shop. Hundreds of silver decorations, jewelry, and dishes lined the walls.

One man chose to buy a silver money clip embellished with a unique design. He used that same money clip for more then twenty-four years. One day the clip finally broke as he placed a few bills inside. Distraught, the missionary ventured back to Baguio and visited the same silversmith school. He explained the situation to a workman and asked him if there was anything that could be done about the broken silver money clip. The workman chuckled as he explained that the design was unique. Only one person could fix the money clip—the original designer. To the missionary's delight, the helpful worker just happened to be the original designer of the broken money clip. With fascination and gratitude, he watched as his silver treasure was perfectly restored.

Each of us is a one-of-a-kind masterpiece of God.

Each of us is a one-of-a-kind masterpiece of God. Because He is our designer, God is the only one who can restore us, and there is nothing we can do that is beyond His restoration. We may think we have done things (or have had things done to us) that are beyond restoration, but God is over the top when it comes to healing, redeeming, and restoring us!

1. Have you ever felt like the broken money clip—damaged or beyond repair? Describe.

2. *When you feel "broken," to whom do you turn for restoration? What does that process look like for you?*

At the Last Supper, before Jesus' crucifixion, Jesus predicted that Peter, one of the disciples, would deny his association with Christ. Peter immediately told Jesus that he would never disown Him (Mark 14:27–31).

3. *However, just as Jesus predicted, Peter denied Christ three times. Read Mark 14:66–72. In the chart below, record the verse in which each denial occurs.*

Denial	Passage
#1	(v. 68)
#2	(v. 70)
#3	(v. 71)

4. *What did Peter do as soon as he heard the rooster crow?*

Peter thought he was disqualified, but Jesus restored him. After His resurrection, Jesus appeared to His disciples several times. The third appearance is described in the Gospel of John.

5. Read *John 21:1–14*. *What did Peter do as soon as he realized Jesus was on the shore (v. 7)?*

6. *What does Peter's response reveal about his desire to be restored by Jesus? If Peter did not want to be restored, how do you think he would have responded?*

7. Read *John 21:15–22*. *How did Jesus restore Peter in this passage?*

8. *Is there anything in your life you believe to be beyond God's restoration or redemption? If so, in the space below, write a prayer to God asking Him to restore you as His masterpiece.*

> *You are a one-of-a-kind masterpiece of God. He has done an amazing work when it comes to creating you. As your designer, God is the only one who can truly restore you when you are damaged or broken.*

Digging Deeper

The prophet Isaiah described the coming Savior as a suffering servant. Isaiah knew He would suffer in order to save us. Read Isaiah 53:5–6. Who is being described in this passage? Who is the One to redeem us all from our iniquities? Who is the One to heal us? Do you think that your healing is out of reach?

Bonus Activity

Look around your house for something that needs restoring. Maybe you have a fence that needs to be painted, a piece of jewelry that needs to be repaired, an appliance that needs to be fixed, or a piece of furniture that needs to be refinished. Put the item on your "to do" list for this week. After it's repaired and restored, spend some time prayerfully thinking about the work of restoration and repair God may want to do in your spiritual life.

Nine

We Can Call upon the Name of Our God

The name Jesus is not only light but food. It is oil without which food for the soul is dry, and salt without which it is insipid. It is honey in the mouth, melody in the ear and joy in the heart. It has healing power. Every discussion where his name is not heard is pointless.

BERNARD OF CLAIRVAUX

Names are an interesting concept. They can tell a lot about a person. They may bring confidence or insecurity, difficulty in explaining the spelling, or trouble correcting the pronunciation. Names are important. In our modern culture, some young moms are turning to celebrities to discover the most popular or unique names. Some people's employment revolves around finding just the right name. That's right—there are people who actually work as baby name consultants!

Today many people choose a name based on its novelty or the way it sounds when spoken. In the past, however, especially in the Jewish culture, a name was chosen based on its meaning. Parents hoped their child would live up to the meaning of the name he or she was given. The names of biblical characters reveal a lot about the people. The next time you read about someone new in the Bible, look up the meaning of his or her name to get to know the person better. You might be surprised by what you discover. A few examples are the names Joshua, Isaac, and David.

The name Joshua means "salvation"; Joshua helped deliver the Israelites to the promised land. The name Isaac means "he laughs"; Abraham and Sarah were filled with joy over the birth of Isaac. Sarah was over ninety and Abraham over one hundred years old when Isaac was born. The name David means "beloved"; this is intriguing because David is described as a man after God's own heart (1 Samuel 13:14).

Sometimes God stepped in and changed people's names. Take this short quiz and see if you can supply each person's changed name.

A New Name Quiz:

Original Name	Changed Name	Scripture Reference	Hint
Abram		Genesis 17:5	He fathered many generations of children.
Sarai		Genesis 17:15	She gave birth when she was over ninety years old!
Simon		Matthew 10:2	He tried to walk on water with Jesus. He is known as the Apostle to the Jews.
Levi		Matthew 9:9; Mark 2:14	The first book of the New Testament is named after him.
Saul		Acts 13:9	He killed Christians before he was saved. He is known as the Apostle to the Gentiles.

While the names of people are important, the names of God used throughout Scripture uncover the very attributes of God. The names of God expose who God is and what God is doing. By studying the names of God, we can get to know Him in deeper ways.

1. *Do you know the meaning of your name? If so, what is the meaning?*

2. *Was there a particular reason you were given your name? Explain.*

Adonai is one of the names for God, and it is used more than three hundred times in the Old Testament. This name is translated as "Lord," written with a capital "L" and lowercase "ord." (This is different from the cap-and-small-caps LORD, which is translated from "Jehovah" or "Yahweh.") Adonai means "Master" or "Lord." The name Adonai is seen for the first time in Genesis 15, when Abram was beginning to be distressed because he had not yet fathered a child—an heir.

3. Read *Genesis 15:1–6*. How did Adonai show His power as Abram's Lord in this passage?

God is all we will ever need. The name El Shaddai is used in the Old Testament almost fifty times. El Shaddai means "God Almighty" or "God All-Sufficient." This is the name of God used by Abraham, Isaac, and Jacob. Even Job used this name to call upon God. The first time El Shaddai was used for God's name appears in Genesis 17:1. The verse reads, "When Abram was ninety-nine years old, the LORD appeared to him and said, 'I am God Almighty [El Shaddai]; walk before me and be blameless.'"

4. Read *Genesis 17:1–8*. Why do you think it was meaningful to Abram that God referred to Himself as "God Almighty"? In what way(s) is it meaningful to you that God is "Almighty" and "All-Sufficient"?

Another name for God is Jehovah-Rohi, which means "the Lord is our Shepherd." Jehovah means "I am and will continue to be," and Rohi means "shepherd." Shepherds are known for their protection and love for their sheep. Psalm 23:1 reads, "The LORD is my shepherd [Jehovah-Rohi], I shall not be in want."

5. Read *Psalm 23*. *How is the Lord your Shepherd? How can accepting God as your Shepherd initiate your surrender of control?*

God decided to send His Son to earth. Jesus is called "Immanuel," which means "God with us." Immanuel is God with skin on. People need a Savior—a God with them.

6. Read *Matthew 1:23*. *In what way has God revealed Himself as "Immanuel" to you? In what ways have you experienced the reality of "God with us"?*

Abba is an informal Aramaic word for "father." While praying before His arrest, Jesus called God "Abba." Rather than using the more formal "Father," Jesus referred to God in the very familiar, childlike sense, much like the term *Daddy* would be used today. Jesus expressed His intimate relationship with His Father as He lamented in Gethsemane. Although this name for God appears only three times in the New Testament, seeing God as your "Abba" is crucial.

7. *Read* **Mark 14:36**. *How does knowing God as your "Daddy" change the way you see and interact with Him?*

8. *When you refer to God, what name do you tend to use (Lord, King, Savior, Provider, etc.)? What does the name you choose to use reveal about His nature?*

Studying the names of God reveals more dimensions of who God is in our world and in our lives.

Digging Deeper

God is a faithful God who never gives up on His people. Read Psalm 9:7–10. In what specific ways have you seen God active and engaged in your life? In what ways have you experienced God as a refuge?

Bonus Activity

Sometime this week, sit down with a piece of paper and a pen. Start listing qualities of God: His names, His attributes, or His promises. Keep this list somewhere safe (maybe in your Bible), to look back on and add to whenever necessary.

Overwhelmed by His Extravagance

God is extravagant with each of us. Not only does
He redeem and restore us, but through Christ we
are made new, we receive a new name, and we are
given a new hope. God is truly over the top with
His love and generosity toward each of us.

Ten

We Are Made New

*God never changes moods or cools off in His
affections or loses enthusiasm. His attitude
toward sin is now the same as it was when He
drove out the sinful man from the eastward
garden, and His attitude toward the sinner the
same as when He stretched forth His hands and
cried, "Come unto me, all ye that labor and
are heavy laden, and I will give you rest."*

A. W. TOZER

December 7, 1941, will live in infamy. Whether or not you or
someone you know lived through it, the attack on Pearl Harbor will
never be forgotten. Mitsuo Fuchida will always remember that day.
Growing up in Japan, Fuchida learned to hate Americans at a young
age. He watched the way many Americans treated Asian immigrants
and was appalled by their behavior and attitude. When the time
came for Fuchida to attend a Japanese military academy, he jumped
at the chance.

In 1941, Fuchida was not only a member of the naval air force of Japan; he had become the nation's top pilot. Mitsuo Fuchida was the one selected to lead the surprise attack on Pearl Harbor. It was Fuchida who uttered the infamous words, "Tora! Tora! Tora!" thereby declaring the attacks victorious. He was the only Japanese officer who survived the attack. Fuchida had another close call during the Battle of Midway in 1942; he was shot down but survived. After hearing about the atomic bomb dropped on Hiroshima, it was Fuchida who sent word of the destruction to the Imperial Command.

There is nothing that God can't make new— including you.

Meanwhile, an American prisoner of war, Jacob DeShazer, found Christ. He had been in captivity due to his part in an air raid on Japanese soil. Instead of being angry and vengeful toward his Japanese captors, DeShazer felt compassion. Following his conversion, he forgave his captors and decided to choose peace over violence from that time forward. Finally, after forty months of confinement, DeShazer was released. Upon his release, he wrote an essay called, "I Was a Prisoner of the Japanese." He later returned to Japan as a missionary and handed out his essay in the form of evangelical pamphlets.

Seven years later, Fuchida was fortunate enough to accept one of the pamphlets, in which DeShazer explained his forgiveness toward the Japanese. Curious, Fuchida later bought and read a Bible, finding and accepting Christ as he read. Fuchida eventually became a world-renowned evangelist to the people of Japan. His life was completely turned around after his encounter with DeShazer's pamphlet.

Like Fuchida, you may be tempted to think there's something in your past that will forever define who you are. You may have been hurt or abused or witnessed an injustice that angered you and made you want vengeance. But the truth is there is nothing that God can't make new—including you. He can transform you from the inside out so that your attitude, actions, responses, and reactions become more like those of Jesus. There is great joy and comfort in knowing that, if you allow Him, God will renew you every day to look a little more like Him.

1. *Have you ever seen a situation you thought was beyond God's restoration, redemption, or ability to make new, yet God surprised you? If so, describe.*

2. *Are there any experiences or encounters from your past in which God renewed and redeemed you? Describe.*

In one of Paul's letters to the church in Corinth, he described the differences that will take place once we accept Christ as our Savior. He asked the believers to treat others as Christ would. In our transformation of newness, we are being formed into the likeness of Christ.

3. Read *2 Corinthians 5:16–21*. Rewrite verse 17 in the space below. Circle or underline the word **new** every time it appears.

4. What does it mean to you to be a new creation in Christ? In what specific ways do you feel like you're a new creation in Christ?

5. *Second Corinthians 5:20* speaks about us as Christ's ambassadors. What are you already doing to fulfill your role as His ambassador?

6. *Are there any changes needed in your life in order to make you more fully and appropriately an ambassador of Christ?*

Not only are we made new creations in Christ, but we are challenged to reflect the light of God's work in us to others.

7. *Read* **Ephesians 4:17–32**. *According to this passage, what does it mean to put on the new self and walk in righteousness and holiness (vv. 25–32)?*

8. *Reflecting on this passage, what are some ways you're being challenged to experience the newness of Christ right now? Is there anything you feel called to change? If so, describe.*

Our God is so over the top—even though He loves us just as we are, He also loves us enough not to leave us there. God is renewing us every day to look more and more like Him.

Digging Deeper

God's renewal is for everyone. Read 2 Corinthians 4:16. How are you outwardly wasting away? Do you feel God's renewal on the inside? Describe.

Bonus Activity

Write a letter to God. It could even be a love letter. Spend time thinking about how you will address God as a friend. Thank Him for making you new. Keep the letter in your Bible or somewhere safe to reflect on in the future.

Eleven

We Receive a New Name

*Within each of us exists the image of God,
however disfigured and corrupted by sin it may
presently be. God is able to recover this image
through grace as we are conformed to Christ.*

ALISTER MCGRATH

In 1920 a man named Subba Rao was born. The name Subba means "snake god." He grew up in the slums of India, where, typically, the name given to a child links the recipient to gods or demons of the Indian culture. God had a different plan for Subba. Subba married a woman named Lydia. She happened to be the daughter of a Lutheran pastor.

Lydia and Subba were married for some years, but Subba had yet to discover Jesus as his personal Savior. He knew bits and pieces of Christianity, but he had never taken the next step of choosing a relationship with God. Lydia and her father prayed long and hard for Subba. Finally, he came to accept Christ. Lydia and her father eventually changed Subba's name to Prasada, meaning "God's gift."

Prasada felt compelled to send the message of Christ into the rural villages surrounding his city, Andhra Pradesh, India, and began a missionary outreach. Through his mission, Prasada sent evangelists to plant churches and extend the love of Christ to all. Now more than 360 villages have been touched by the work of Prasada.

Like Prasada, many Indians who choose to become Christians receive a new name when they are baptized. Instead of keeping the names that are often tied to gods of the Indian culture, they exchange them for Christian names. Through their decision to receive Christ in their lives, they sever ties to their old lives. The newly granted names signify the journey of a new life.

When we become followers of God and His children, our identity completely changes.

Although Americans are rarely called by a new name upon receiving Christ, make no mistake—Christ gives us a new name. Revelation 2:17 says, "He who has an ear, let him hear what the Spirit says to the churches. To him who overcomes, I will give some of the hidden manna. I will also give him a white stone with a new name written on it, known only to him who receives it." In this verse, the "hidden manna" refers to the food that kept the Israelites alive before their entrance into the promised land. The "white stone" refers to the token received by victors in challenges or games during the time John wrote Revelation. Winners of the Greek games or gladiator competitions would receive a white stone symbolizing their victory. God's gifts, as referred to in this verse, are rewards for those who show faithfulness to God.

The name God gives us reveals God's great love for each of us. It also shows us that when we become followers of God and His children, our identity completely changes. We are literally transformed from the inside out.

1. *What would you like your new, God-given name to be?*

2. *Not only does Christ give us a new name, but we are given a new identity in Christ. Match Scripture below with the appropriate description of who we are in Christ.*

Scripture Reference	Who I Am in Christ
John 1:12	I am justified.
Romans 5:1	I am a citizen of heaven.
Philippians 3:20	I am complete in Christ.
Ephesians 2:10	I am a child of God.
Colossians 2:9–10	I am God's workmanship.

3. *Do you tend to think of yourself in terms of the descriptions in these passages? Why or why not?*

4. How do you respond to being called "justified," "God's child," and "God's workmanship"?

5. How do these truths change the way you see yourself? How might they change the way you choose to live?

6. Fill in the chart using the Scriptures in the left column to reveal other facets of who you are in Christ.

Scripture	Who I Am in Christ
Matthew 5:14	I am the light of the world.
Romans 1:6	
John 15:15	
1 Corinthians 12:27	
John 15:5	

7. Do you tend to think of yourself in terms of the descriptions in these passages? Why or why not?

8. How does realizing your identity in Christ change the way you reflect Christ to those around you?

Not only does the Bible tell us we are given a new name in Christ, but we are also given a new identity through Jesus.

Digging Deeper

Upon believing in Christ, we are given not only a new name, but also a new heart. Read Ezekiel 11:19. What is the reason for a change in behavior after we accept Christ as our Savior? What does an "undivided heart" look like to you?

Bonus Activity

Make a list of the names of your family members and friends. Look up their names on a baby name Web site or in a baby name book. Write down their meanings. You might be surprised to find similarities between the person and the meaning of his or her name.

Twelve

We Receive a New Hope

*In God alone is there faithfulness and faith
in the trust that we may hold to him, to his
promise, and to his guidance. To hold to
God is to rely on the fact that God is there
for me, and to live in this certainty.*

KARL BARTH

While reading the morning newspaper on May 2, 1962, Vincent Hallinan stumbled upon a rather unusual advertisement posted in the classified section. It read: "I don't want my husband to die in the gas chamber for a crime he did not commit. I will therefore offer my services for ten years as a cook, maid, or housekeeper to any leading attorney who will defend him and bring about his vindication."

As one of the city's most famous lawyers, Hallinan was moved by the woman's heartfelt cry for help. He contacted the woman and discovered her husband was about to face trial for killing an antiques dealer. The husband's fingerprints had been found on the bloodstained sword used in the murder, and the prosecutors were confident of a guilty verdict. After completing long and hard research, Hallinan was able to prove the husband's fingerprints were left on the sword during a shopping visit to the store with a friend.

In the end, he was able to prove that the man had not killed the antiques dealer. Hallinan was declared innocent. Faithful to her promise, the woman was ready to fulfill her commitment to service, but Hallinan refused the offer. Both the woman and her husband had been set free.

Many times in our lives we feel hopeless. Like the woman in this story, we are desperate to get the help we need. Thankfully, God is our hope. Not only does God demonstrate that He is over the top in His love, grace, mercy, and patience, but He also fills us with the contagious gift of hope.

> *Not only does God demonstrate that He is over the top in His love, grace, mercy, and patience, but He also fills us with the contagious gift of hope.*

1. *Have you ever been in a desperate situation when hope seemed lost? What did you do? How did you respond?*

2. *To whom do you turn during difficult times when hope seems lost?*

Jesus knew He was going to die in order to save the world from sin. In the Upper Room, Jesus reminded the disciples five times that they wouldn't be alone.

3. Read **John 16:12–16**. What hope did Jesus give to His followers in this passage?

4. Within your faith journey, what is your source of hope? Where do you find your comfort?

5. Read **Colossians 1**. How do you think the recipients felt after receiving this portion of the letter from Paul?

6. Reflecting on **Colossians 1**, make a list of the reasons mentioned or alluded to within this chapter for the hope of a believer.

7. Reflecting on your list, which things fill you with the most hope?

8. What steps can you take to share the hope of God with others more every day?

*God fills us with hope through the promises
found in the Bible. Not only can we find
our hope renewed by what God has already
done, but also by what is still to come.*

Digging Deeper

In his letter to the Roman church, Paul pleaded with the Romans to unite as one body for Christ—Jews and Gentiles. Read Romans 15:13. With what did Paul ask God to fill the people? Of what significance is it for you to have a "God of hope"?

Bonus Activity

Have you ever considered making a prayer list? Start today! Write down all the people, situations, joys, and struggles that you pray for. Then you have not only a way to keep track of every prayer, but also a way to keep a testimony of God's faithfulness over time.

Leader's Guide

Chapter 1: Popping with Surprises

Focus: *God is over the top when it comes to His love for you. His work in and through you is greater than anything you can imagine.*

1. *We've all had kitchen mishaps—from the blender whose top wasn't on tight enough to the pan that boiled over onto everything. Use this question as an icebreaker to get participants talking, sharing, and laughing.*

2. *This question is designed to invite participants to share a moment when God made Himself real to them in everyday life. Some may share stories of moments of comfort or encouragement from God. Others may describe an awareness of His presence or a sense of His call to pray for someone.*

3. *Answers will vary. This icebreaker question is designed to allow the group a chance to reveal times in their lives when they have seen God moving in powerful and explosive ways.*

4. *Paul prayed that the people would be strengthened through Christ and that Christ would dwell within them. He prayed that they would begin to understand the love Christ had for them. Many people want to fully understand the love of Christ. Encourage participants to use this passage as a prayer for themselves and their loved ones.*

5. *Paul said that God is greater than and works beyond our wildest imaginations. He can "do immeasurably more than all we ask or imagine."*

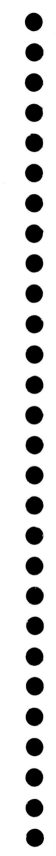

6. *Answers will vary, but God works in abounding ways for His children. He truly does do more than we can even ask or imagine.*

7. *We can limit God's involvement and activity in our lives in a variety of ways. Fear, doubt, bitterness, anger, and unforgiveness can all hold us back from the things God wants to do in our lives.*

8. *Some participants may recall someone they need to forgive. Others may be challenged to spend more time in prayer or studying the Bible. Answers will vary widely on this question, but encourage women to take action on whatever they mention.*

Digging Deeper

God (or Christ) gave Paul strength to do all he accomplished. Answers will vary. Many people may not have been afraid or discouraged, but strengthened, when they considered God as their rock and source of their strength.

Chapter 2: Coloring Outside the Lines

Focus: *God wants us to walk in wholeness. In His love, God wants to erase every line that separates us from Him.*

1. *Answers will vary. Participants may have lines (limits or boundaries) in their hearts that hinder their relationships with God and with others.*

2. *Answers will vary, but disappointment, unanswered prayers, and anger at God can all cause us to draw lines in our relationships with Him.*

3. *Answers will vary. Drawing lines in a relationship with God will hurt the relationship, make us less vulnerable and intimate with Him, and cause us to be less likely to pray and less likely to serve, give, and love others. These attitudes hurt God and us.*

4. *Answers will vary, but include: honest, transparent, and vulnerable.*

5. *Answers will vary. There is no place we can go where God will not be. He has no limits. For some, this may be comforting and encouraging. Others may find it frightening or deterring.*

6. *Answers*

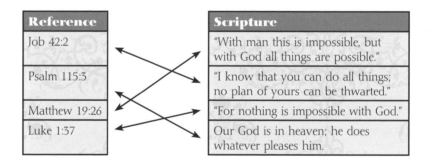

Reference	Scripture
Job 42:2	"With man this is impossible, but with God all things are possible."
Psalm 115:3	"I know that you can do all things; no plan of yours can be thwarted."
Matthew 19:26	"For nothing is impossible with God."
Luke 1:37	Our God is in heaven; he does whatever pleases him.

7. *Drawing lines in a relationship with God is never healthy. God, in His infinite power and might, gives us a choice as to whether we will choose to fully submit ourselves to Him. He could overpower us, but He allows us to choose. However, in His love, He will nudge us along the way.*

8. *Answers will vary, but by confronting this question, we can begin to ask God for the wisdom, grace, and courage to erase some of the lines we draw in our relationships with Him.*

Digging Deeper

Answers will vary, but many seek God's comfort. In times of fear or struggle, experiencing God's presence is often a source of comfort and peace.

Chapter 3: Grace Abounding

Focus: *Grace is a free gift from God that cannot be earned or purchased. Through grace, not only do we have the opportunity to enter into a relationship with God, but we are saved and empowered to do good works.*

1. *Answers will vary, but people may be amazed by grace shown through someone in an unlikely position to extend that kind of action. It's also interesting that La Guardia still honored the law and the justice system; he just did it in a way that was laced with kindness and generosity.*

2. *Answers will vary. Everyone was probably in shock that a man of such high stature stooped down to show grace to a lowly woman. The vendor was probably upset and angry. The woman was most likely humbled and thankful.*

3. *Encourage participants to share their own stories of having a debt forgiven or an opportunity granted that was completely undeserved. Often, receiving something we don't deserve (like grace) is humbling and fills us with gratitude.*

4. *"But when the <u>kindness</u> and <u>love</u> of God our Savior appeared, he saved us, not because of righteous things we had done, but because of his <u>mercy</u>. He saved us through the washing of rebirth and renewal by the Holy Spirit, whom he poured out on us generously through Jesus Christ our Savior, so that, having been justified by his <u>grace</u>, we might become heirs having the hope of eternal life."*

5. *While everyone's responses will vary, many find it difficult to accept the free gift of grace. Some may not feel worthy of God's grace; others may struggle to believe that God's grace is really free. Yet God loves us so much that He sent His Son to die for us, giving us the opportunity for eternal life and an ongoing relationship with Him.*

6. *"But because of his great <u>love</u> for us, God, who is rich in <u>mercy</u>, made us alive with Christ even when we were dead in transgressions—it is by <u>grace</u> you have been saved. And God raised us up with Christ and seated us with him in the heavenly realms in Christ Jesus, in order that in the coming ages he might show the incomparable riches of his <u>grace</u>, expressed in his <u>kindness</u> to us in Christ Jesus. For it is by <u>grace</u> you have been saved, through faith— and this not from yourselves, it is the gift of God—not by works, so that no one can boast."*

7. *Because grace is a gift, we cannot attain it through works or on our own. Thus, we can never boast that it's our own accomplishment. Knowing grace is a gift from God makes us more dependent on Him.*

8. *Grace is for everyone. We can extend grace by expressing kindness, forgiveness, and gentleness even when those receiving it don't exhibit grace themselves.*

Digging Deeper

According to Paul, God's grace has been lavished on us with all wisdom and understanding. By living a life of grace, we are called to forgive the unforgivable and love the unlovable—just as God does for us.

Chapter 4: For God So Loved the World

Focus: *God so loves the world that nothing is beyond His redemption or restoration. Like the father in the story of the prodigal son, God is a forgiving Father who wants to see us come home to a relationship with Him.*

1. *Answers will vary, but this question will encourage participants to share moments when they've reached out to someone less fortunate than themselves. It will also challenge them to reflect on how their faith and life were strengthened by the experience.*

2. *Answers will vary, but this question will challenge participants to reflect on their own times of need and the importance of community.*

3. Answers

Person	Reaction
Younger Son	(vv. 18–19) He may have felt humbled and embarrassed that it had come to this, but ultimately joyous that his father accepted him with open arms instead of turning away.
Father	(v. 20) He ran to his son, hugging him and kissing him. He even threw a huge party in honor of his prodigal son! He was excited to have his son back, no matter the circumstances.
Older Brother	(vv. 28–30) He was jealous. He never left his father's side over the years and didn't feel as welcomed as his prodigal little brother. He may have felt angry and bitter toward his father and especially toward his brother.
Servants	(vv. 22–24) They may have been shocked at the son's return and the father's reaction. They may have seen how distraught the father was when the son left and assumed he would be angry and spiteful at his return, but the exact opposite happened!

4. Answers will vary, but most of us can relate to the characters in this story in one way or another.

5. He allowed his son to make his own decisions.

6. Answers will vary. We all face temptation and the lure that the grass is greener elsewhere, but just as the young son experienced, the grass is rarely greener elsewhere. Unfortunately, choosing to take everything and run hurts others and us.

7. *Answers will vary. We have all made bad decisions, but it's important to highlight that nothing is beyond God's redemption and restoration. Encourage participants by reminding them that God does work everything for good for those who love Him and are called according to His purposes. That does not mean there are not consequences for our poor decisions, but it does mean that God can restore and renew.*

8. *God gives us the opportunity to make choices. In the foolish moments when we squander what He has given us through poor choices or self-destructive behavior, He still waits each day for our return into His loving arms.*

Digging Deeper

Nicodemus asked Jesus about salvation and the meaning of being born again. Jesus came to save the world—all of humanity that exists in the darkness. He did not come just to save the Jews, but to save everyone, even those of us who don't feel worthy. While not everyone accepts the gift of His work on the cross, God wants everyone to be reconciled to Him.

Chapter 5: Multidimensional Love

Focus: *God's love is multidimensional.*
His love isn't just given to us; it's meant
to flow through us to others.

1. *Answers will vary. Have the group consider the impoverished, homeless, orphaned, and lonely in their communities.*

2. *Answers will vary but could include such reactions as wonderful, awe-inspiring, unexplainable, or powerful. Everyone is eligible to receive this love—no one is exempt!*

3. *Answers*

Scripture	Description of God's Love
John 15:13	It is a self-sacrificing love!
Romans 8:35	Nothing can separate us from His love!
John 14:23	It is intimate!
Ephesians 6:24	We can receive grace through His love!
Jeremiah 31:3	God's love is inviting!

4. *Answers will vary. Ask participants to share their favorites from the Scriptures above and add other Scriptures about God's love that they appreciate. Examples could include John 3:16; 1 Corinthians 13; and 1 John 4.*

5. *The priest and religious leader may not have wanted to get involved or to become unclean. They may have been in a hurry or been fearful they would also be attacked if they stopped to help the man.*

6. "But a Samaritan, as he _traveled_, _came_ where the man was; and when he _saw_ him, he _took_ pity on him. He _went_ to him and _bandaged_ his wounds, _pouring_ on oil and wine. Then he _put_ the man on his own donkey, _took_ him to an inn and _took_ care of him. The next day he _took_ out two silver coins and _gave_ them to the innkeeper. 'Look after him,' he said, 'and when I return, I will _reimburse_ you for any extra expense you may have.'"

7. Answers will vary, but it's interesting to note the Samaritan paid for the man's recovery but didn't stay to personally care for him. It appears he did everything within his ability at the time, but he could not stay several weeks to ensure the man's recovery. In our modern society, a person others could be tempted to look down upon based on his or her background, socioeconomic status, or reputation would be comparable to the Samaritan in the story.

8. By showing mercy to others, living generously, and recognizing that our neighbors may need us in inconvenient times, we behave as the good Samaritan did. Countless ways exist to show God's multidimensional love toward others.

Digging Deeper

Jesus commands in Luke 10:27: "Love the Lord your God with all your heart and with all your soul and with all your mind and with all your strength." By loving Him with our hearts, souls, minds, and strengths, we can fully express our love with all we are: our thoughts, words, and actions.

Chapter 6: Uncontainable Love

Focus: *God's love is uncontainable. It's meant to flow out of our lives in every direction—even when we least expect it. When we experience God's love personally, we're in the best place to share His love with others.*

1. *Answers will vary. Have the participants share their results as a group. This quiz and accompanying questions are designed to allow participants to warm up to the topic and one another.*

2. *Answers will vary. It is difficult to show uncontainable love in situations where you don't feel love in return: in a fight with a spouse or family member, in the workplace, under stress, or around those who make you feel uncomfortable. On the other hand, it may be easier to show uncontainable love in church, toward your spouse, your children or family members, or toward those whom you don't know as well.*

3. *Nothing can be accomplished without love. Paul declared that nothing he said could be heard or understood without love. He asserted that, even should he possess all the faith in the world, without love he was nothing. He further stated that giving everything to the poor meant nothing without love.*

4. *Answers*

Love is . . .	Love is not . . .
Patient	Envious
Kind	Boastful
Rejoicing in truth	Proud
Protecting	Rude
Trusting	Self-seeking
Hoping	Easily angered
Preserving	A keeper of wrongs
	Something that delights in evil
	Failing

Replacing the word **love** *with the name of Jesus makes this passage more personal. The Greek word for* **love**, **agape**, *describes a love made possible only by God. By replacing* **love** *with* **Jesus**, *we can more clearly understand the endless love found through our Savior.*

5. *Faith, hope, and love remain. Paul might have chosen love as the greatest of the three because it is the foundation of Christianity. Through love, Christ was sent to erase our sins and give us eternal life.*

6. *The love of Christ surpasses knowledge. It's often hard to wrap our minds around the love of God.*

7. *Answers will vary. By allowing Christ access to our lives so that He may dwell in us, we are rooting ourselves in love. Christ is love.*

8. *Answers will vary. Through prayer and studying God's Word, we will be surrounded by evidence of God's love. By rooting ourselves in His love, we can learn to reflect that love in our actions, thoughts, and words toward others.*

Digging Deeper

We are asked to "bear with each other and forgive whatever grievances you may have against one another. Forgive as the Lord forgave
you. And over all of these virtues put on love, which binds them all
together in perfect unity." By putting on love (which is the root of
all), we can look past our grievances with one another and forgive
just as God has forgiven us.

Chapter 7: Amazingly Generous

Focus: *God is amazingly generous to each
of us, and we have the opportunity to reflect
that generosity to others. God does not want
us to give out of guilt or compulsion, but
with a cheerful heart that honors Him.*

1. *Answers will vary. This icebreaker question may lead to some fun
   discussions on movies, Newman's acting career, or even favorite
   salad dressings.*

2. *By allowing the participants a chance to reveal their passions,
   they may begin networking. There are remarkable nonprofits all
   over the world that need assistance. The need isn't always funding
   (although that does help). Consider giving your time to your
   favorite nonprofit.*

3. Answers

God's Overwhelming Actions
(v. 3) Blessed us in the heavenly realms with every spiritual blessing in Christ
(v. 4) Chose us in Him before the creation of the world to be holy and blameless in His sight
(v. 5) Predestined us to be adopted as His children through Jesus Christ
(v. 6) Freely gave us grace in the One He loves
(v. 7) Redeemed us through His blood
(v. 8) Lavished grace upon us with all wisdom and understanding
(v. 9) Made known to us the mystery of His will according to His good pleasure

4. *Answers will vary. Many times we get caught up in daily life and forget to think about all God has done for us. Encourage participants to intentionally set aside time to remind themselves of all God has done for them.*

5. *Answers will vary. The participants may have seen God work through money issues, love issues, faith issues, or other difficult times. Have the group share their experiences.*

6. *We are to receive abounding grace (v. 8). Also, verses 10 and 11 tell us we will be made rich in every way so that we can always be generous.*

7. *Answers will vary, but there is an unmistakable joy that comes when we give.*

8. *Answers will vary but may include giving more toward a church or another organization of choice with a happy and content heart.*

Digging Deeper

Jesus delivers the needy who cry out, has compassion for the weak, and saves the needy. Answers will vary, but many participants may have felt like the weak, needy, or afflicted described in this passage. The outcomes may also vary greatly. Remind the participants that God is our provider; however, not every one of our pleas is answered the way we want.

Chapter 8: Nothing Is Beyond Restoration

Focus: *You are a one-of-a-kind masterpiece of God. He has done an amazing work when it comes to creating you. As your designer, God is the only one who can truly restore you when you are damaged or broken.*

1. *Answers will vary. This question is an intimate one, and some participants may choose to share tender moments from their past or present. Respond with compassion and try to avoid trying to "fix" the person or situation.*

2. *Ideally, we should turn to God for restoration; but often we try to find comfort in other sources, some of which are unhealthy, including gambling, addiction, or inappropriate relationships.*

3. Answers

Denial	Passage
#1	(v. 68) "But he denied it. 'I don't know or understand what you're talking about,' he said."
#2	(v. 70) "Again he denied it."
#3	(v. 71) "I don't know this man you're talking about."

4. *Peter remembered what Jesus had told him: "Before the rooster crows twice you yourself will disown me three times" (v. 30). He then wept because he had disowned Jesus. He thought his denial was unforgivable.*

5. *Peter (also known as Simon Peter) grabbed his clothes and jumped into the water, swimming to Jesus. He wanted to get there as quickly as possible.*

6. *Peter showed that he still deeply desired a relationship with Jesus, even after his denials. He was eager to reconnect with Jesus. If Peter didn't want to be restored, then he might have waited for the boat to come to shore or maybe even stayed in the boat.*

7. *Jesus challenged Peter by asking him about his love. Three times Peter affirmed that he really loved Jesus. Then Jesus told Peter what would happen to him in his old age. It wasn't a pretty picture. But the calling of Jesus remained the same: "Follow me."*

8. *There is nothing beyond God's restoration or redemption, although we may feel otherwise. God is the ultimate Restorer. He is over the top in His forgiveness and redemption.*

Digging Deeper

Jesus. Jesus. Jesus. He was sent by God to die for our sins. Nothing can separate us from the love of Christ. He is the source of our healing and restoration.

Chapter 9: We Can Call upon the Name of Our God

Focus: Studying the names of God reveals more dimensions of who God is in our world and in our lives.

A New Name Quiz:

Original Name	Changed Name	Scripture Reference	Hint
Abram	Abraham	Genesis 17:5	He fathered many generations of children.
Sarai	Sarah	Genesis 17:15	She gave birth when she was over ninety years old!
Simon	Peter	Matthew 10:2	He tried to walk on water with Jesus. He is known as the Apostle to the Jews.
Levi	Matthew	Matthew 9:9; Mark 2:14	The first book of the New Testament is named after him.
Saul	Paul	Acts 13:9	He killed Christians before he was saved. He is known as the Apostle to the Gentiles.

1. *Encourage each member of the group to share the meaning of her name. This question is designed to get the group laughing and sharing.*

2. *Encourage each member of the group to share the origin of her name. This question is designed to get the group laughing and sharing.*

3. *Verse 2 reads, "Abram said, 'O Sovereign LORD [Adonai], what can you give me since I remain childless and the one who will inherit my estate is Eliezer of Damascus?'" In verse 1, God told Abram not to fear, for He was his shield and reward! God reminded Abram of His power and pointed to the stars in the sky, promising Abram children as numerous as those stars.*

4. *Abraham was about to have the profound experience of entering a covenant with God. God promised Abraham something Abraham could not do on his own; only God could bring it to fruition. At that moment, Abraham needed to know that God was almighty—He was enough, He was sufficient. Thousands of years later, we still need to know that God is enough and sufficient.*

5. *Answers will vary. The Lord is our Shepherd because He is in control and is leading us away from our fears and troubles. By trusting the Lord as our Shepherd, we can let go. We can release our fears and troubles and rest in our Shepherd's arms.*

6. *The verse reads, "The virgin will be with child and will give birth to a son, and they will call him Immanuel'—which means, 'God with us.'" Answers will vary, but God has been with each of us, even in times when we didn't realize His presence.*

7. This verse reads, "'Abba, Father,' he said, 'everything is possible for you. Take this cup from me. Yet not what I will, but what you will.'" Seeing God as "Daddy" ushers us into a more intimate relationship with Him; we begin to see Him, not just as Master or Lord, but as Father.

8. Answers will vary. Challenge the group to use a less-familiar name of God this week during their prayer time.

Digging Deeper

Answers will vary. By seeking God, we learn that He will never leave us or forsake us. We can find our comfort and safety in Him.

Chapter 10: We Are Made New

Focus: *Our God is so over the top—even though He loves us just as we are, He also loves us enough not to leave us there. God is renewing us every day to look more and more like Him.*

1. Answers will vary, but encourage participants to share stories of healing and restoration in the lives of people they know. This can be an encouraging and uplifting time of sharing.

2. This question is more personal. Some participants may not feel comfortable sharing experiences and stories from their past.

3. The verse reads, "Therefore, if anyone is in Christ, he is a _new_ creation; the old has gone, the _new_ has come!"

4. *By becoming new in Christ, we are no longer of this world. We also have a greater hope than ever before. Living in Christ gives us a new perspective on everything.*

5. *Answers will vary. Our goal is to demonstrate and be a witness of the good news to others. We can do this through service, kindness, love, prayer, and actively sharing the good news with others by our words and our lifestyles.*

6. *Answers will vary, but desired changes may include being more outspoken about one's faith, praying more regularly, studying the Bible in-depth, or looking for opportunities to put one's faith into practice.*

7. *We are asked to speak only the truth, refuse to go to bed angry, not steal, not speak unwholesomely, and not be bitter, angry, or slanderers. Instead, we are to show kindness and compassion to one another.*

8. *Answers will vary, but some participants may feel they need to work on being wiser with their words, forgiving others, or choosing to show grace and forgiveness even in difficult situations.*

Digging Deeper

Every day we are getting older. Our bodies will eventually waste away. However, on the inside, we can be renewed by God every single day.

Chapter 11: We Receive a New Name

Focus: *Not only does the Bible tell us we are given a new name in Christ, but we are also given a new identity through Jesus.*

1. *Answers will vary. Consider checking out a book of baby names from the local library or searching for names online. Remember, in some traditions children are named because the parents have a particular hope or preferred destiny for their child.*

2. *Answers*

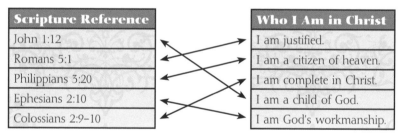

Scripture Reference	Who I Am in Christ
John 1:12	I am justified.
Romans 5:1	I am a citizen of heaven.
Philippians 3:20	I am complete in Christ.
Ephesians 2:10	I am a child of God.
Colossians 2:9–10	I am God's workmanship.

3. *Answers will vary. It is not uncommon to be unlikely to think of oneself in these terms. Since we all live in the world, we tend to describe ourselves in worldly terms instead of how we are seen by God.*

4. *Answers will vary. Participants may feel overwhelmed or blessed by their new identities in Christ.*

5. *Answers will vary, but participants may see themselves in a better light through knowing how God sees them.*

6. Answers

Scripture	Who I Am in Christ
Matthew 5:14	I am the light of the world.
Romans 1:6	I am among the called of Jesus Christ.
John 15:15	I am a friend of Christ.
1 Corinthians 12:27	I am a member of the body of Christ.
John 15:5	I am a branch of the true vine.

7. Some may easily identify with these descriptions while others may not. Many participants may already know their identity in Christ, but for those who don't, these Scriptures can be a great reminder of the love Christ has for them.

8. Answers will vary. By realizing we are made new by Christ, we can reflect those traits to the world around us.

Digging Deeper

Our hearts are being replaced. In place of a heart of stone, we receive a heart of flesh. Answers will vary, but a godly, undivided heart is a heart that pledges all allegiance and loyalty to God.

Chapter 12: We Receive a New Hope

Focus: *God fills us with hope through the promises found in the Bible. Not only can we find our hope renewed by what God has already done, but also by what is still to come.*

1. *Answers will vary. Many have been through trials when hope was needed. The trials may have been problem friendships or relationships, experiencing the death of a loved one, or work issues. Whatever the problem, when we cling to the hope of God, we will be fulfilled.*

2. *Answers will vary. During hard times, many turn to God in prayer or seek help from family members, longtime friends, and even neighbors.*

3. *This passage is full of hope and promise. Jesus said the Spirit of Truth—the Holy Spirit—would come and guide them. The Holy Spirit made Jesus known since He was physically gone. Jesus also promised that we would see Him again.*

4. *Answers will vary, but God's Spirit is a source of comfort and hope. The Holy Spirit fills us with hope for Christ's return. We can find hope in many promises throughout Scripture.*

5. *We can only imagine, but the people of Colosse probably felt built up, encouraged, and full of hope.*

6. *Answers will vary. Grace and peace are given by God our Father. Faith, love, and hope come from heaven. The gospel continues to grow all over the world. We are rescued from the dominion of darkness and brought into the kingdom of Jesus. We have redemption and the forgiveness of sins with Jesus. God created all. We were once enemies of God, but we have been reconciled through the cross.*

7. *Answers will vary. Some tend to find their hope in what God has done while others tend to find their hope in what God will yet do.*

8. *By choosing to live life with hope, you can radiate that hope to those around you. The hope granted to you by God is not limited to just you but can be enjoyed by everyone around you. One great way to spread the hope of God is to simply share with others what He is doing in your life.*

Digging Deeper

Paul asked God to fill the people with joy and peace. Having a God of hope means there is always hope. God's hope is eternal; we never need to live in unhealthy fear or be without hope.

About the Author

Margaret Feinberg is an author and speaker who offers a refreshing perspective on faith and the Bible. She has written more than a dozen books, including *The Organic God* and *God Whispers*. She also wrote the Women of Faith Bible study *Overcoming Fear*. Margaret is a popular speaker at women's events, luncheons, and retreats as well as national conferences, including Catalyst, LeadNow, Fusion, and the National Pastors Conference.

She lives in Lakewood, Colorado, in the shadow of the Rockies, with her six-foot-eight husband, Leif. When she's not writing and traveling, she loves hiking, shopping, blogging, laughing, and drinking skinny vanilla lattes with her girlfriends. But some of her best days are spent communicating with her readers.

So if you want to put a smile on her face, go ahead and write to her!

Margaret@margaretfeinberg.com
www.margaretfeinberg.com
www.margaretfeinberg.blogspot.com

Tag her on Facebook or follow her on Twitter:
www.twitter.com/mafeinberg

WOMEN OF FAITH

presents

2 Days of
Inspiration for Women

At a Women of Faith weekend, you'll join thousands of other women for a surprisingly intimate, unexpectedly funny, deeply touching 2-day event. Renowned speakers, award-winning musical artists, best-selling authors, drama, and more combine for a hope-filled event like no other.

> The music was incredible and each speaker's message either brought me to tears, laughing, or both! I have never had a more fulfilling, uplifting experience! You rehabilitated my soul! —Debbie

Coming to a City Near You

Schedule, Talent line up, and more at **womenoffaith.com**
Or call **888.49.FAITH** for details.

Join us at One of These Life-Changing Events!

It's the perfect getaway weekend for you and your friends—or a special time just for you and God to share. **Register Today!**

WOMEN OF FAITH®
womenoffaith.com | 888.49.FAITH
Women of Faith events are productions of Thomas Nelson Live Events.

WOMEN OF FAITH®
presents

Imagine
WOMEN OF FAITH®

WOMEN OF FAITH®
over
the top

Two Tours. 29 Cities.
Countless Lives Changed.

Join us at one of these life-changing events!
See when we'll be in your area. Go to **womenoffaith.com** for current schedule and talent lineup.

Imagine Coming to:

Billings, MT
April 9–10, 2010

Denver, CO
September 24–25, 2010

Las Vegas, NV
April 23–24, 2010

Phoenix, AZ
October 1–2, 2010

Omaha, NE
August 13–14, 2010

Portland, OR
October 8–9, 2010

Dallas, TX
August 20–21, 2010

San Antonio, TX
October 22–23, 2010

Tulsa, OK
August 27–28, 2010

Seattle, WA
October 29–30, 2010

Anaheim, CA
September 10–11, 2010

Kansas City, MO
November 5–6, 2010

Spokane, WA
September 17–18, 2010

Sacramento, CA
November 12–13, 2010

Over the Top Coming to:

Des Moines, IA
March 12–13, 2010

Milwaukee, WI
October 1–2, 2010

Shreveport, LA
April 23–24, 2010

Rochester, NY
October 8–9, 2010

Columbus, OH
April 30–May 1

Tampa, FL
October 15–16, 2010

Indianapolis, IN
August 20–21, 2010

St. Paul, MN
October 22–23, 2010

Washington DC
August 27–28, 2010

Ft. Lauderdale, FL
November 5–6, 2010

Philadelphia, PA
September 10–11, 2010

Greensboro, NC
November 12–13, 2010

Cleveland, OH
September 17–18, 2010

Hartford, CT
November 19–20, 2010

Atlanta (Duluth), GA
September 24–25, 2010